Executive Summary

President Obama's FY 2013 Budget proposes a bold plan to renew and expand America's infrastructure. The plan includes a $50 billion up-front investment connected to a $476 billion six-year reauthorization of the surface transportation program and the creation of a National Infrastructure Bank. In support of this commitment, the Department of the Treasury, with the Council of Economic Advisers, has updated our analysis of the economic effects of infrastructure investment. The new data and analyses confirm and strengthen our finding that now is an ideal time to increase our investment in infrastructure for the following four key reasons:

- Well-designed infrastructure investments have long-term economic benefits and create jobs in the short run;
- This economic activity and job creation is especially timely as there is currently a high level of underutilized resources that can be used to improve and expand our infrastructure;
- Middle-class Americans would benefit disproportionately from this investment through both the creation of middle-class jobs and by lowering transportation costs for American households; and
- There is strong demand by the public and businesses for additional transportation infrastructure capacity.

Return on Investment

- Many studies have found evidence of large private sector productivity gains from public infrastructure investments, in many cases with higher returns than private capital investment. Research has shown that well-designed infrastructure investments can raise economic growth, productivity, and land values, while also providing significant positive spillovers to areas such as economic development, energy efficiency, public health, and manufacturing.

- However, not every infrastructure project is worth the investment. Investing wisely in infrastructure is critically important, as is facilitating private financing for public infrastructure. Traditional funding methods limit the flexibility and cost-effectiveness of infrastructure financing. For example, there is currently very little direct private investment in our nation's highway and transit systems due to the current method of funding infrastructure, which lacks effective mechanisms to attract and repay direct private investment in these types of infrastructure projects.

- Newer funding initiatives address some of these funding shortcomings. The establishment of a National Infrastructure Bank would enable greater private sector co-investment in infrastructure projects. A National Infrastructure Bank would also allow for the rigorous analysis required to direct support to projects with both the greatest returns to society and the long-run economic benefits that can justify up-front investments.

- Build America Bonds (BABs) were another highly successful tool to attract additional private capital to finance infrastructure projects. These bonds were used to fund over $180 billion for new public infrastructure such as bridges, transit systems, and hospitals from 2009 through 2010 in all 50 states and the District of Columbia. Reinstatement of the BABs program is proposed in the President's Budget.

Investing in Infrastructure Uses Underutilized Resources

- Among those who gain employment as a result of additional infrastructure investment, the average unemployment rate has averaged approximately 13 percent over the past twelve months. This is more than one and one-half times the current national unemployment rate. Within the construction sector, which accounts for the majority of direct employment resulting from infrastructure investment, the unemployment rate has averaged 15.6 percent over the past twelve months.

- Construction costs and other costs associated with building projects are especially low in the current environment. As a result, the President has taken decisive action to accelerate project permitting and environmental review. In the President's August 31, 2011 Memorandum, he directed the heads of all executive departments and agencies to: "(1) identify and work to expedite permitting and environmental reviews for high-priority infrastructure projects with significant potential for job creation; and (2) implement new measures designed to improve accountability, transparency, and efficiency through the use of modern information technology. Relevant agencies should monitor the progress of priority projects; coordinate and resolve issues arising during permitting and environmental review; and develop best practices for expediting these decisions that may be instituted on a wider scale, consistent with applicable law." In addition, in this year's State of the Union address, the President announced his intention to "sign an executive order clearing away the red tape that slows down too many construction projects."

Supporting the Middle Class

- Investing in transportation infrastructure creates middle-class jobs. Our analysis suggests that 61 percent of the jobs directly created by investing in infrastructure would be in the construction sector, 12 percent would be in the manufacturing sector, and 7 percent would be in the retail and wholesale trade sectors, for a total of 80 percent in these three sectors. Nearly 90 percent of the jobs in these three sectors most affected by infrastructure spending are middle-class jobs, defined as those paying between the 25th and 75th percentile of the national distribution of wages.

- The President's proposal emphasizes transportation choices, including mass transit and high-speed rail, to deliver the greatest long-term benefits to those who need it most: middle-class families. The average American family spends more than $7,600 a year on transportation, which is more than they spend on food and more than twice what they spend on out-of-pocket health care costs. For 90 percent of Americans, transportation costs absorb one out of every seven dollars of income. This burden is due in large part to the lack of alternatives to expensive and often congested automobile travel. Multi-modal transportation investments are critical to making sure that American families can travel without wasting time and money stuck in traffic.

- A more efficient transportation infrastructure system will reduce our dependence on oil, saving families time and money. Traffic congestion on our roads results in 1.9 billion gallons of gas wasted per year, and costs drivers over $100 billion in wasted fuel and lost time. More efficient air traffic control systems would save three billion gallons of jet fuel a year, translating into lower costs for consumers. Finally, new research indicates that Americans who were able to live in "location efficient" housing were able to save $200 per month in lower costs, including paying less at the pump, over the past decade.

Americans Want More Transportation Investment

- After years of underinvestment in our transportation system, Americans' satisfaction with our public transit system is middling when compared to public satisfaction with highways and public transit systems around the world. We rank 15th out of 32 OECD nations with respect to our satisfaction with our roads and highways. We are tied with four other countries at rank 13 (out of 32 OECD nations) with respect to our satisfaction with public transit.

- One study found that four out of every five Americans agree with the statement that: "In order for the United States to remain the world's top economic superpower, we need to modernize our transportation infrastructure and keep it up to date." Another study found that almost 19 out of 20 Americans are concerned about America's infrastructure and 84 percent support greater investment to address infrastructure problems.

An Economic Analysis of Infrastructure Investment

I. Introduction

President Obama's FY 2013 Budget proposes a bold plan to renew and expand America's infrastructure. This plan includes a $50 billion up-front investment connected to a six-year $476 billion reauthorization of the surface transportation program and the creation of a National Infrastructure Bank. The President's plan would significantly increase investment in surface transportation by approximately 80 percent when compared to previous federal investment. The plan seeks not only to fill a long overdue funding gap, but also to reform how Federal dollars are spent so that they are directed to the most effective programs. This report contributes to the ongoing policy dialogue by summarizing the evidence on the economic effects of investments in transportation infrastructure.

Public infrastructure is an essential part of the U.S. economy. This has been recognized since the founding of our nation. Albert Gallatin, who served as President Jefferson's Treasury Secretary, wrote: "The early and efficient aid of the *Federal* Government is recommended by still more important considerations. The inconveniences, complaints, and perhaps dangers, which may result from a vast extent of territory, can no otherwise be radically removed or prevented than by opening speedy and easy communications through all its parts. Good roads and canals will shorten distances, facilitate commercial and personal intercourse, and unite, by a still more intimate community of interests, the most remote quarters of the United States. No other single operation, within the power of Government, can more effectually tend to strengthen and perpetuate that Union which secures external independence, domestic peace, and internal liberty."[1]

Gallatin spoke in terms of infrastructure shortening distances and easing communications, even when the only means to do so were roads and canals. Every day, Americans use our nation's transportation infrastructure to commute to work, visit their friends and family, and travel freely around the country. Businesses depend on a well-functioning infrastructure system to obtain their supplies, manage their inventories, and deliver their goods and services to market. This is true for companies whose businesses rely directly on the infrastructure system, such as shippers like UPS and BNSF, as well as others whose businesses indirectly rely on the infrastructure system, such as farmers who use publicly funded infrastructure to ship crops to buyers, and internet companies that send goods purchased online to customers across the world. A modern transportation infrastructure network is necessary for our economy to function, and is a prerequisite for future growth. President Eisenhower's vision is even more relevant today than it was in 1955, when he said in his State of the Union Address, "A modern, efficient highway

---

[1] Williamson, John, "Federal Aid to Roads and Highways Since the 18th Century: A Legislative History" Congressional Research Service, January 6, 2012.

system is essential to meet the needs of our growing population, our expanding economy, and our national security." Today, that vision would include making not only our highways, but our nation's entire infrastructure system more efficient and effective.

Our analysis indicates that further infrastructure investments would be highly beneficial for the U.S. economy in both the short and long term. First, estimates of economically justifiable investment indicate that American transportation infrastructure is not keeping pace with the needs of our economy. Second, because of high unemployment in sectors such as construction that were especially hard hit by the bursting of the housing bubble, there are underutilized resources that can be used to build infrastructure. Moreover, states and municipalities typically fund a significant portion of infrastructure spending, but are currently strapped for cash; the Federal government has a constructive role to play by stepping up to address the anticipated shortfall and providing more efficient financing mechanisms, such as Build America Bonds. The third key finding is that investing in infrastructure benefits the middle class most of all. Finally, there is considerable support for greater infrastructure investment among American consumers and businesses.

The President's plan addresses a significant and longstanding need for greater infrastructure investment in the United States. Targeted investments in America's transportation infrastructure would generate both short-term and long-term economic benefits. However, transforming and rehabilitating our nation's transportation infrastructure system will require not only greater investment but also a more efficient use of resources, because simply increasing funding does not guarantee economic benefits. This idea is embodied in the President's proposal to reform our nation's transportation policy, as well as to establish a National Infrastructure Bank, which would leverage private and other non-Federal government resources to make wise investments in projects of regional and national significance.

In this report, we begin by reviewing factors that should influence investment in infrastructure. We review the economic literature regarding returns to infrastructure investment. Next, we consider the specific condition of our economy and labor market, including the availability of workers with the requisite skills, which suggest that now is a particularly favorable time to initiate these investments. Then we analyze the benefits derived by American families and companies from well-functioning infrastructure systems and the costs associated with poor infrastructure systems. Finally, we review public and business sentiment regarding infrastructure investment.

II.   Economic Benefits from Investing in Infrastructure

The United States has a rich history of investing in infrastructure and reaping the long-term economic benefits. Influential research by David Aschauer and others has explored the link between public infrastructure investment and economic growth.[2,3,4] Aschauer's research and numerous other studies have found evidence of large private sector productivity gains from public infrastructure investments, in many cases with higher returns than private capital investment. Since much of the public capital stock is owned by state and local authorities, more recent research has compared the economic benefits of infrastructure investments between regions in the United States, generally finding smaller but economically significant benefits in comparison to Aschauer's estimates.[5]

Investments in infrastructure allow goods and services to be transported more quickly and at lower costs, resulting in both lower prices for consumers and increased profitability for firms. Major transportation infrastructure initiatives include the building of the national railroad system in the 19th century and the creation of the Eisenhower Interstate System in the 1950s and 1960s. Observers have concluded that in both of these cases there was a causal link running from infrastructure investments to subsequent private sector productivity gains.[6] Alternatively, it is possible that infrastructure investments occur when productivity gains are also likely to follow but for unrelated reasons. Determining causality is difficult.

A study by John Fernald makes progress on establishing causality by comparing the impact of infrastructure investment on industries that *a priori* should experience different benefits from infrastructure spending.[7] He finds that the construction of the interstate highway system in the 1950s and 1960s corresponded with a significant increase in the productivity of vehicle-intensive industries (such as transportation and gas utilities), relative to industries that do not depend on vehicles (such as apparel and textiles and industrial machinery). Fernald's findings suggest that previous investments in infrastructure led to substantial productivity gains, and highlight the potential for further increases in productivity through additional, well-targeted investments.

---

[2] Aschauer, David. "Is Public Expenditure Productive?" J. Monet. Econ., Mar. 1989a, 23(2), pp. 177-200.
[3] Aschauer, David. "Public Investment and Productivity Growth in the Group of Seven," Econ. Perspectives, 1989b, 13(5), pp. 17-25.
[4] Aschauer, David. "Does Public Capital Crowd Out Private Capital?" J. Monet. Econ., 1989c, 24(2), pp. 171- 88.
[5] Munnell, Alicia H, 1992. "Infrastructure Investment and Economic Growth," Journal of Economic Perspectives, American Economic Association, vol. 6(4), pages 189-98, Fall.
[6] Munnell, Alicia H, 1992. "Infrastructure Investment and Economic Growth," Journal of Economic Perspectives, American Economic Association, vol. 6(4), pages 189-98, Fall.
[7] Fernald, John G., "Roads to Prosperity? Assessing the Link Between Public Capital and Productivity," *The American Economic Review,* Vol. 89, No. 3 (Jun., 1999), pp. 619-638.

Building a National Community

The advent of railroads in the 19th century brought time standardization to the United States. Before rail travel was available, cities and towns across America set their clocks based on local sunrises and sunsets. However, the lack of time coordination across cities caused rail travelers considerable confusion.[8]

To address this issue, railroad managers developed the current nationwide time system with four distinct time zones to allow for a uniform schedule for arrivals and departures. Thus, the development of rail lines furthered the goal of a national community by allowing people and goods to travel quickly from one place to another, reducing the time to travel across the country from five to six months to just five days, and by leading to the development of a national time standard.

Just as the development of railroads provided greater opportunities for Americans, boosted economic productivity, and helped build a national community, increased investment in transportation infrastructure can provide these same benefits today. Research has found significant benefits from increased agglomeration of people, firms, and industrial activity, particularly in manufacturing.[9] Strategic investments in infrastructure can help connect Americans in new ways to sustain communities and increase economic growth.

Edward Gramlich argues that the greatest return on investment can be garnered from spending on the maintenance of existing highways.[10] Citing data from the Congressional Budget Office, he finds an extremely high rate of return from bringing road conditions up to their minimum state of good repair. Interestingly, he also finds that improvements beyond the state of good repair are not associated with positive returns. Allocating maintenance dollars to where they are most needed is likely to generate high rates of return and improve safety, suggesting that our spending on infrastructure should prioritize funding maintenance where roads are in disrepair. This is consistent with the Administration's "fix-it-first" proposal which emphasizes repairing existing infrastructure.

Not surprisingly, the literature suggests that the economic benefits from various infrastructure projects vary widely.[11,12] Moreover, even if previous infrastructure investments had economic

---

[8] Mintz, S. (2007). "Building the Transcontinental Railroad."*Digital History*. Retrieved October 6, 2010 from <http://www.digitalhistory.uh.edu/database/article_display.cfm?HHID=177>.

[9] Edward L. Glaeser, Ed. Agglomeration Economics. Chicago: University of Chicago Press, 2010.

[10] Gramlich, Edward, "Infrastructure Investment: A Review Essay," *Journal of Economic Literature*, Vol. 32, No. 3 (Sept., 1993), pp. 1176-1196.

[11] Gramlich, Edward, "Infrastructure Investment: A Review Essay," *Journal of Economic Literature*, Vol. 32, No. 3 (Sept., 1993), pp. 1176-1196.

benefits, it is not clear that policymakers should expect the same rate of return for subsequent infrastructure investments. This is especially true when one considers the network effects that are associated with the creation of original transportation networks. We must continue to take advantage of new investment opportunities made available by technological progress and be mindful of the fact that at some point, there are diminishing returns from further investments in a particular area. As Fernald observed, "Building an interstate network might be very productive; building a second network may not."[13]

In addition to the positive impact on economic growth and productivity, there are other benefits from infrastructure investments. Available evidence suggests that infrastructure investment can raise property values, which reflects an improvement in living standards. For example, research suggests that proximity to public transit raises the value of residential and commercial real estate. Bernard Weinstein studied the effect of the Dallas light rail system on property values, and found that a jump in total valuations around light rail stations was about 25 percent greater than in similar neighborhoods not served by the system.[14] This is consistent with studies conducted in St. Louis,[15] Chicago,[16] Sacramento,[17] and San Diego,[18] all of which find that property values experience a premium effect when located near public transit systems. Research has also shown that broadening the definition of housing affordability to include transportation costs reduces the number of effectively affordable neighborhoods in the United States; thus, infrastructure investment which lowers transportation costs should help increase access to homeownership.[19]

A study by Climent Quintana-Domeque and Marco Gonzalez-Navarro makes progress on estimating the causal effect of infrastructure investment on property values, using an experimental design.[20] Specifically, the study randomly assigned some roads to be paved and others to be in a control group in the Mexican city of Acayucan. Their analysis suggests that

[12] Gramlich, for example, cites CBO data that demonstrate different rates of return across different types of infrastructure investments, including new construction and maintenance.

[13] Fernald, John G., "Roads to Prosperity? Assessing the Link Between Public Capital and Productivity," *The American Economic Review,* Vol. 89, No. 3 (Jun., 1999), pp. 619-638.

[14] Weinstein, B. et al. "The Initial Economic Impacts of the DART LRT System." Center for Economic Development and Research, University of North Texas, 1999.

[15] Garrett, T. "Light Rail Transit in America: Policy Issues and Prospects for Economic Development," Federal Reserve Bank of St. Louis, 2004.

[16] Gruen, A."The Effect of CTA and METRA Stations on Residential Property Values." Regional Transportation Authority, 1997.

[17] Landis, J. et al. "Rail Transit Investments, Real Estate Values, and Land Use Change: A Comparative Analysis of Five California Rail Systems." Institute of Urban and Regional Development, UC Berkeley, 1995.

[18] Cervero, R. et al. "Land Value Impacts of Rail Transit Services in San Diego County," Urban Land Institute, 2002.

[19] Housing and Transportation Affordability Index, Center For Neighborhood Technology (CNT), February 28, 2012. Housing affordability is traditionally defined as housing cost less than 30 percent of an area's median income; the broader definition is housing plus transportation costs together comprise less than 45 percent of median income.

[20] Quintana-Domeque, Climent and Marco Gonzalez-Navarro, "Street Pavement: Results from an Infrastructure Experiment in Mexico," Industrial Relations Section, Princeton University, Working Paper No. 556, (Jul., 2010).

such infrastructure investment substantially raised housing values on the newly paved roads, as well as provided benefits for home values on nearby streets. The rise in housing values on affected streets significantly exceeded the cost of paving the roads.

The benefits from transportation infrastructure extend beyond its effects on property values and housing affordability. For example, in Chicago, transportation agglomeration benefits have led to greater business clustering and economic growth associated with manufacturing, as businesses took advantage of Chicago's position in a national transportation network.

Finally, a well-maintained and robust network of transportation infrastructure, which allows individuals to access multiple modes of transportation, results in significant efficiency benefits for Americans. One study found that in 2009, households at the national median level of income residing in "location efficient" neighborhoods with diverse transportation choices realized over $600 in transportation cost savings, compared to similar households living in less efficient areas.[21] Further, well-maintained roads with adequate capacity, coupled with access to public transit and other driving alternatives, can lower traffic congestion and accident rates which not only saves Americans time and money but also saves lives. Congestion is not limited only to our nation's roads but also to our rails. Freight rail systems can play a vital role in relieving road traffic and in moving goods in a more fuel efficient manner. One study estimated that on average, freight railroads are four times more fuel efficient than trucks.[22] These benefits can also reduce dependence on foreign oil, improve energy efficiency, and reduce air pollution. For example, one study in the Los Angeles area found that traffic congestion has a significant effect on CO_2 emissions, and that reducing stop-and-go traffic conditions could potentially reduce emissions by up to 12 percent.[23] Another study estimates that America's public transportation system reduces gasoline consumption by 4.2 billion gallons annually. [24]

---

[21] Housing and Transportation Affordability Index, Center For Neighborhood Technology, February 28, 2012.
[22] Association of American Railroads, Freight Railroads Help Reduce Greenhouse Gas Emissions, November 2011.
[23] Barth, Matthew and Kanok Boriboonsomsin. "Real-World CO2 Impacts of Traffic Congestion." University of California at Riverside, 2008. <http://www.uctc.net/papers/846.pdf>.
[24] American Public Transit Association, "Facts at a Glance, 2012".
<http://www.publictransportation.org/news/facts/Pages/default.aspx>.

Creating a More Livable Community

Infrastructure investment should create a more livable community for working Americans. The Department of Transportation, Department of Housing and Urban Development, and the Environmental Protection Agency have formed the Partnership for Sustainable Communities, which has identified six principles for improving the lives of working families:

- **Provide more transportation choices** to decrease household transportation costs, reduce our dependence on oil, improve air quality, and promote public health.

- **Improve economic competitiveness of neighborhoods** by giving people reliable access to employment centers, educational opportunities, services, and other basic needs.

- **Target federal funding toward existing communities** – through transit-oriented development and land recycling – to revitalize communities, reduce public works costs, and safeguard rural landscapes.

- **Align federal policies and funding** to remove barriers to collaboration, leverage funding, and increase the effectiveness of programs to plan for future growth.

- **Enhance the unique characteristics of all communities** by investing in healthy, safe and walkable neighborhoods, whether rural, urban, or suburban.

- **Expand location- and energy-efficient housing choices** for people of all ages, incomes, races, and ethnicities to increase mobility and lower the combined cost of housing and transportation. To this end, the U.S. Department of Housing and Urban Development (HUD) is working with private sector firms to develop a Housing and Transportation Affordability (HTA) Index that measures the combined cost of housing and transportation as a share of household income.
  - The HTA index will help inform transportation infrastructure investment decisions and housing assistance programs by highlighting areas where investment may be expected to have the highest payoff.
  - This work is especially important given that from 2000 to 2009, housing and transportation costs increased by almost 40 percent, surpassing growth in median national income (see footnote 19).

III.   Why Now?

The first part of this report demonstrated that additional, carefully selected infrastructure investment should yield substantial benefits to the U.S. economy. This section considers the current state of our economy and why it is an opportune time to increase infrastructure investment. The main conclusion is that because of the availability of underutilized resources (especially labor), the opportunity cost of infrastructure investment is currently well below its normal level.

The recession that started in late 2007 had an exceptionally large impact on the labor market, as the United States lost 8.7 million jobs between December 2007 and December 2009. Due to the collapse of the real estate market, the contraction of employment in the construction industry was especially acute. A full 21 percent of those who lost jobs over this time period were in the construction industry.

Even as the economy has begun to recover, construction employment remains well below pre-recession levels. In December 2011, total payroll jobs in the construction industry remained 25 percent below the level of December 2007, dropping 1.9 million from 7.5 million to 5.6 million employees (seasonally-adjusted), which constitutes one-third of the total jobs lost over this period. In February 2012, the unemployment rate for construction workers was 17.1 percent, and over the past twelve months, the unemployment rate for construction workers has averaged 15.6 percent.

Building more roads, bridges, and rail tracks would especially help those workers that were disproportionately affected by the economic crisis – construction and manufacturing workers. Accelerated infrastructure investment would provide an opportunity for construction workers to productively apply their skills and experience. Moreover, hiring currently unemployed construction workers would impose lower training costs on firms than would be incurred by hiring workers during normal times because these workers already have much of the requisite skills and experience. Analysis by the Congressional Budget Office found that additional investment in infrastructure is among the most effective policy options for raising output and employment.[25] Given this situation, the President's proposal to front-load our six-year surface transportation legislation with an additional $50 billion investment makes sound economic sense.

There are other factors that make current construction especially timely and costs low, translating into lower project costs. This impact on project costs is well-illustrated by the Federal Aviation Administration's experience awarding $1.1 billion in Recovery Act funds for airport improvements. The money was designated for 300 projects. The winning bids for those projects

---

[25] Congressional Budget Office, "Policies for Increasing Economic Growth and Employment in the Short Term," January 2010.

came in over $200 million below the engineers' estimates. A second round of projects was selected, which also received lower bids than anticipated. As a result of these cost savings, 367 runway and airport improvement projects were funded with the money that was originally intended to support 300 projects.

The states and transit authorities that selected most of the highway ($26.6 billion) and transit ($8 billion) projects supported by the Recovery Act reported similar experiences, and similar bid savings. Overall, the Department of Transportation (DOT) estimates that more than 2,000 additional airport, highway, bridge, and transit projects were funded because of low bids or projects being completed under budget.

NextGen

NextGen is also a timely initiative. American air travelers lose substantial time due to congestion, flight delays, cancellations and missed connections. The total cost of these delays to passengers was estimated at $16 billion in 2007. Problems in our aviation system result in significant cost increases to airlines as well, with an estimated $8 billion in increased costs.[26] Adopting a next generation air traffic control system (NextGen) could significantly reduce these delays and their associated costs. NextGen would help both the Federal Aviation Administration and airlines to install new technologies and, among other improvements, move from a national ground-based radar surveillance system to a more accurate satellite-based surveillance system – the backbone of a broader effort to reduce delays for passengers, increase fuel efficiency for carriers, and cut airport noise for those who live and work near airports. According to one study, implementation of NextGen technology would result in a reduction of 4 million hours of passenger delay annually, savings of 3 billion gallons of fuel, and the elimination of 29 million metric tons of carbon emissions. Total projected savings from NextGen implementation would result in $29 billion of net benefits annually for the United States by 2026.[27] These benefits justify the President's request to increase federal investment in NextGen to over $1 billion in fiscal year 2013.

In addition, the President is making it easier for states and localities to undertake infrastructure projects by accelerating project permitting and environmental review by federal departments and agencies. The August 31, 2011 Presidential Memorandum directed the heads of all executive departments and agencies to: "(1) identify and work to expedite permitting and environmental reviews for high-priority infrastructure projects with significant potential for job creation; and (2) implement new measures designed to improve accountability, transparency, and efficiency

---

[26] National Center of Excellence for Aviation Operations Research (NEXTOR), "Total Delay Impact Study," November 2010.
[27] Deloitte, "Transforming the Air Transportation System," 2011.

through the use of modern information technology. Relevant agencies should monitor the progress of priority projects; coordinate and resolve issues arising during permitting and environmental review; and develop best practices for expediting these decisions that may be instituted on a wider scale, consistent with applicable law". In addition, in this year's State of the Union address, the President announced his intention to "sign an executive order clearing away the red tape that slows down too many construction projects."

Another critical question is whether there are worthwhile infrastructure projects available for investment at this time. While well-targeted infrastructure investment can be tremendously beneficial, experience has also shown that poorly targeted infrastructure investments have limited or even negative effects in the long run. The Recovery Act established the Transportation Investment Generating Economic Recovery (TIGER) program to spur a national competition for innovative, multi-modal, and multi-jurisdictional transportation projects that promise significant economic and environmental benefits to an entire metropolitan area, region, or the nation. As part of the open competition for this investment, the Department of Transportation conducted a solicitation for projects meeting the TIGER criteria, providing a test case to determine the supply of these kinds of infrastructure projects. TIGER's purpose is to select projects that improve roads, bridges, rail, ports, public transit, and inter-modal facilities.

Since its inception, TIGER allocated $2.6 billion to 172 competitively selected projects. The demand for TIGER co-investment has been tremendous. DOT has received applications from 3,248 projects, from all 50 states and the District of Columbia. Combined, these projects requested over $90 billion in federal funding, with many projects also supported by state, local, and sometimes private capital. For the most recent round of TIGER funding DOT has received more than 1,000 applications requesting $13 billion in funding for innovative infrastructure projects. TIGER has also maintained its selectivity, which is the basis for sound investments: with an acceptance rate of only 5 percent, TIGER is more selective than admission into Harvard University's freshman class.

Enhancing the efficiency of existing infrastructure is also a critical component of the President's plan. As noted earlier, research has shown that investment that improves existing infrastructure networks can have significant returns. The Recovery Act also created the Transit Investments in Greenhouse Gas and Energy Reduction (TIGGER) program to support such improvements by providing public transit agencies with one-time grants to improve the energy efficiency of their existing operations. Increasing energy efficiency for transportation is particularly important since the transportation system accounts for one-third of all carbon dioxide emissions from fossil fuel combustion, the largest share of any economic sector in the United States, according to Environmental Protection Agency estimates.[28] The cost of energy is a significant factor in the

---

[28] "Frequent Questions – Emissions." U.S. Environmental Protection Agency, 2010.
<http://epa.gov/climatchange/fq/emissions.html>.

cost of providing public transportation; one study found that the cost of providing public transportation rises by $7.6 million for every penny increase in the price of gasoline.[29]

Since its establishment, the TIGGER program has received $225 million in funding. During those three years, the Federal Transit Administration (FTA) has received applications for 889 projects with a total value of over $3.45 billion, fifteen times larger than the amount of available funding. FTA has been able to award TIGGER grants to 88 competitively selected projects.

Finally, it is important to consider the economic situation facing state and local governments who are significant partners in funding public infrastructure. During recessions, it is common for state and local governments to cut back on capital projects – such as building schools, roads, and parks – in order to meet balanced budget requirements. At the beginning of the most recent recession, tax receipts at the state and local level contracted for four straight quarters; receipts are still below pre-recession levels. Past research has found that expenditures on capital projects are more than four times as sensitive to year-to-year fluctuations in state income as is state spending in general.[30] However, the need for improved and expanded infrastructure is just as great during a downturn as it is during a boom. Providing immediate additional federal support for transportation infrastructure investment would be prudent given the ongoing budgetary constraints facing state and local governments, the upcoming reduction in federal infrastructure investment as Recovery Act funds are depleted, and the strong benefits associated with public investment.

Build America Bonds (BABs) are an excellent example of a program that has been highly successful at stimulating infrastructure investment. Introduced as part of the Recovery Act, BABs are taxable bonds issued by state and local governmental or public entities. The Federal government pays a 35 percent direct subsidy to the issuer to offset the additional borrowing costs associated with issuing taxable debt. BABs had a very strong reception from both issuers and investors. From the inception of the program in April 2009 to when it expired on December 31, 2010, there were 2,275 separate BABs issues, which supported more than $181 billion of financing for new public capital infrastructure projects. State and local governments saved an estimated $20 billion in borrowing costs, on a net present value basis, from issuing BABs. On average, a Build America Bonds issuer saved 84 basis points on interest costs for 30-year bonds and also received significant savings on shorter maturities, as compared to traditional tax-exempt bonds.[31]

---

[29] "Impact of Rising Fuel Costs on Transit Services." American Public Transportation Association, May 2008. <http://www.apta.com/resources/reportsandpublications/Documents/fuel_survey.pdf>.

[30] James R. Hines, Hilary Hoynes, and Alan Krueger, "Another Look at Whether a Rising Tide Lifts All Boats," in *The Roaring `90s: Can Full Employment Be Sustained?*, edited by Alan B. Krueger and Robert Solow, Russell Sage and Century Fund, 2001.

[31] Treasury Department Analysis of Build America Bonds, May 2011.

BABs were successful for a variety of reasons. Because they are taxable bonds, they broadened the set of investors interested in holding municipal debt to include pension funds and other long-term institutional investors that do not have tax liabilities, as well as middle-class taxpayers who would not receive the full benefit from tax-exempt debt. This is significant as the traditional tax-exempt bond market is approximately $2.8 trillion, while the broader conventional taxable bond market is roughly $30 trillion. Second, BABs are a more efficient way to deliver the existing federal subsidy for state and local government borrowing. The subsidy for traditional tax-exempt bonds is widely considered to be inefficient because federal revenue costs are greater than the benefits that state and local governments receive in lower borrowing costs.[32]

All 50 states, the District of Columbia, and two territories participated in this voluntary program. One example of a successful project financed by BABs is the expansion of the Parkland Health and Hospital System which is part of the Dallas County Hospital District. Dallas County voters approved a plan in 2008 to replace the current hospital with a new, state-of-the-art facility. When it came time to finance this important project, BABs were a significant source of funding. One analysis found that, "the utilization of BABs as compared to a structure of only tax-exempt bonds is estimated to have resulted in a net present value savings to Dallas County taxpayers of more than $119 million."[33] The issuance was so successful that it was recognized as the Deal of the Year in the Southwest by *The Bond Buyer*.

---

[32] See "Subsidizing Infrastructure Investment with Tax-Preferred Bonds," CBO/JCT, October 2009.
[33] Case Study conducted by First Southwest Company: <http://publicfinance firstsw.com/case-study/show/46/>.

The Role of a National Infrastructure Bank

There are improvements that can be made in how we finance infrastructure investment. Governments on all levels face significant budget constraints. It is imperative that we maintain and strategically grow our investments in key areas, such as infrastructure, and finding additional sources of capital would increase our ability to do so, while also increasing efficiency in our project selection process.

President Obama has proposed a National Infrastructure Bank to help finance infrastructure projects. A well-designed infrastructure bank could:

• increase overall investment in infrastructure by attracting private capital to co-invest in specific infrastructure projects;
• improve the efficiency of our infrastructure investment by having a merit-based selection process for projects; and
• fill the gaps in our infrastructure funding system, which currently disadvantage investments in multi-modal and multi-jurisdictional infrastructure projects.

One way to address the need for more infrastructure investment is to attract more private capital for direct investment in transportation infrastructure. There is currently very little direct private investment in our nation's highway and transit systems. The lack of private investment in infrastructure is in large part due to the current method of funding infrastructure, which lacks effective mechanisms to attract and repay direct private investment in specific infrastructure projects. In addition, the private benefit for investors is less than the benefit for society as a whole because of positive externalities from infrastructure. A National Infrastructure Bank could address these problems by directly funding selected projects through a variety of means. The establishment of a National Infrastructure Bank would create the conditions for greater private sector co-investment in infrastructure projects.

Additionally, with a few notable exceptions, federal funding for infrastructure investments is not distributed on the basis of a competition between projects using rigorous economic analysis or cost-benefit comparisons. The current system virtually ensures that the distribution of investment in infrastructure is suboptimal from the standpoint of raising the productive capacity of the economy.

To address the lack of merit-based funding, a National Infrastructure Bank would develop a framework to analytically examine potential infrastructure projects using a cost-benefit analysis, and would evaluate the distributional impact of both the costs and benefits of each project. Of course, not all costs and benefits from infrastructure projects can be quantified, but an effort should be made to quantify those that can be quantified and to take account of any additional benefits and costs to society. A rigorous analytical process would result in support for projects that yield the greatest returns to society, and would avoid investing taxpayer dollars in projects where total costs exceed total societal benefits. A National Infrastructure Bank would select projects along a sliding scale of support that most effectively utilizes the bank's limited resources, targeting the most effective and efficient investments.

IV.   <u>How Infrastructure Investment Affects the Middle Class</u>

For the average American family, transportation expenditures rank second only to housing expenditures. As can be seen in Figure 1, the average American annually spends more on transportation than food, and more than two times as much as on out-of-pocket healthcare expenses. Given how much Americans spend on transportation expenditures, public investments which lower the cost of transportation could have a meaningful impact on families' budgets. Reducing fuel consumption, decreasing the need for car maintenance due to potholes and poor road conditions, increasing the availability of affordable and accessible public transit systems, and reducing fuel consumption by making better use of the land would benefit Americans and allow them to spend less money on transportation.

Figure 1.

For the 90 percent of Americans who are not among the top decile in the income distribution, transportation costs absorb one out of every seven dollars of income. Transportation expenses relative to income are almost twice as great for the bottom 90 percent as they are for the top 10 percent.

Figure 2.

Providing high-speed rail and improved public transportation would provide middle-class families with more options to save time and money, so that they can retain more of their income for other purposes and spend more time doing what they want, rather than spending time getting there. One study concluded that individuals in a two-person household who ride public transportation and eliminate one car save, on average, almost $10,000 annually.[34] Improved

---

[34] American Public Transportation Association, *Transit Savings Report,* July 14, 2011. See appendix 1 for cities with greatest savings. <http://www.apta.com/mediacenter/pressreleases/2011/Pages/110714_Transit_Savings.aspx>.

accessibility to public transportation systems will also help protect household budgets against the impact of rising fuel costs over time. For example, research has estimated that between 2000 and 2009, median income households living in neighborhoods with diverse transportation choices and regional accessibility experienced a $200 per month savings in average transport costs, compared to similar households in less location efficient areas.[35]

Moreover, improving our nation's transportation system can save middle-class families money by reducing the costs associated with congestion and the additional automobile maintenance caused by poor road conditions. One study found that poor conditions of roads cost the average motorist who drives in cities on a regular basis over $400 a year.[36,37] Another study by the Department of Transportation finds that $85 billion in total investment per year over the next twenty years would be required in order to bring existing highways and bridges into a state of good repair.[38] As Gramlich and others have found, these fix-it-first investments will save money for most American families.

Infrastructure Investment Creates Middle-Class Jobs

Spending on infrastructure generates demand for products and services from a variety of industries. For example, road building not only requires construction workers, but also grading and paving equipment, gasoline or diesel to run the machines, a variety of smaller hand tools, raw inputs of cement, gravel, and asphalt, surveyors to map the site, engineers and site managers, and even accountants to keep track of costs.

Data from the Commerce Department's Bureau of Economic Analysis (BEA) provide insight into how a dollar's worth of demand for some broad categories of spending is divided among the supplying industries. Analysis of data from the BEA 2010 annual input-output table and related data from the Bureau of Labor Statistics (BLS) on the composition of industry employment suggests that 61 percent of the jobs created by investing in infrastructure would be in the construction sector, 12 percent would be in the manufacturing sector, and 7 percent would be in retail trade, for a total of 80 percent in these three sectors. Using BLS data on the structure of occupations in those industries, and the distribution of wages for those occupations by industry, nearly 90 percent of the jobs in the three sectors most affected by infrastructure spending are middle-class jobs, defined as those between the 25th and 75th percentile in the national distribution of wages.

---

[35] Housing and Transportation Affordability Index, Center For Neighborhood Technology, February 28, 2012.
[36] America's Roughest Rides and Strategies to Make Our Roads Smoother, Sept. 2010.
<www.tripnet.org/urban_roads_report_Sep_2010.pdf>.
[37] See appendix 2 for a chart of 20 urban areas where costs are the highest.
[38] Department of Transportation, 2010 Status of the Nation's Highways, Bridges and Transit: Conditions and Performance Report.

Further analysis suggests that the jobs created by investing in infrastructure are not only middle-class jobs, but also are concentrated in occupations and industries that have been disproportionately affected by the recent economic downturn. Overall, the unemployment rate among those who would be put to work by additional investment in infrastructure has averaged approximately 13 percent over the past twelve months, more than one and one-half times the current national unemployment rate.[39]

Figure 3.

One example of this can be found in Lincoln, Nebraska. Most people would never guess that an investment in improving the New York City transit system would create middle-class manufacturing jobs in Lincoln. However, that is exactly what happens every time New York's MTA or Metro North buys a rail car made at the Kawasaki factory in Lincoln. This factory, Kawasaki USA's largest manufacturing plant, employs over 1,000 workers. The plant was established in 1974 as a consumer products center and expanded in 2001 to build rail cars. The vast majority of new M-8 rail cars ordered by New York Transit's Metro North System (340 out of 382) are made in this plant, meaning that most of the folks who commute from Connecticut to

---

[39] Treasury calculations using most recent Bureau of Labor Statistics data.

New York City by rail have ridden or will ride on a car made in this plant. [40] This is another example of the geographic diversity of benefits which comes from investing in infrastructure.

The Costs of Underinvesting in Infrastructure

Although infrastructure investments are expensive, it is even more expensive to skimp on infrastructure. There are real costs of failing to invest in infrastructure, including increased congestion and foregone productivity and jobs. Already, Americans are wasting too much time, money, and fuel stuck in traffic. The Texas Transportation Institute (TTI) recently estimated that Americans in 439 urban areas spent some 4.8 billion hours sitting in traffic in 2010, equivalent to nearly one full work week for the average commuter. TTI's calculations suggest that congestion caused Americans to purchase an extra 1.9 billion gallons of fuel, costing over $100 billion in wasted time and added fuel costs in the 439 urban areas it surveyed.[41]

The United States' infrastructure system benefits working families by reducing transportation costs and increasing efficiency. While traffic jams are one of the universal features of our infrastructure system, they do tend to occur at peak commuting hours. Those who are on the road then tend to be working Americans and the costs are often greatest for those who are on fixed schedules. We should continue to invest in infrastructure so working Americans can continue to accrue these benefits.

---

[40] <http://www.mta.info/mnr/html/newM8 html>.
[41] Urban Mobility Report 2011, Texas Transportation Institute, September, 2011.
<http://tti.tamu.edu/documents/mobility-report-2011.pdf/>,
<http://mobility.tamu.edu/ums/report/congestion_cost.pdf>.

An Analytic Approach for Measuring Congestion

Although Texas Transportation Institute's estimate is a good benchmark when evaluating congestion costs, it is important to remember that it is not always clear that time spent in congestion should be valued at the wage rate. A key input for achieving an efficient allocation of resources along a sliding scale is a rigorous measure of congestion severity across regions. Two such measures are available. The Texas Transportation Institute has developed the well-known Travel Time Index (TTI) which quantifies the ratio of total travel time in the peak period over uncongested travel time in the peak period (commute time under free flow traffic conditions); the higher the TTI index, the larger the share of peak travel time that is subject to congestion. The TTI is independent of the total amount of peak travel – it simply measures the fraction of peak hours subject to delay because of congestion. In contrast, CEOs for Cities[42] uses an alternative measure – total peak travel time, which unlike the TTI index, captures the effects of urban sprawl (but does not have anything to say about what fraction of peak commute time is affected by congestion). These approaches complement each other. For example, the two metrics can first be normalized to the same 0-1 scale (because the units of measure are different). Next, a simple average of the normalized metrics can be taken to form a hybrid index that reflects both urban sprawl and congestion intensity, and which can then be used to rank locations along a sliding scale.

The Department of Transportation recommends using a variety of values of time to evaluate the economic costs, depending on whether the travel takes place as part of paid business travel, local commuting travel, or long-distance leisure travel. The value of time in freight transportation is even more complex, varying with the value and perishability of the cargo that is being transported. Additionally, there are costs of congestion beyond lost time and wasted fuel. For example, a recent survey by Gallup found that those with long commutes are more likely to experience back and neck pain. Studies of economic well-being have found that time spent commuting is among the most stressful and least enjoyable of daily activities.[43] Moreover, congestion leads to more rapid road erosion and higher maintenance costs, a higher frequency of accidents and associated need for emergency services, higher pollution per car, and productivity losses from traffic delays. All of these potential costs of congestion – and corresponding benefits of alleviating congestion – should be factored into any cost-benefit analysis of infrastructure alternatives that would relieve congestion.

---

[42] " Measuring Urban Transportation Performance – A Critique of Mobility Measures and a Synthesis", Joe Cortright, Impresa and CEOs for Cities, September 2010.

[43] Kahneman, Daniel, et al. 2004. "A Survey Method for Characterizing Daily Life Experience: The Day Reconstruction Method." *Science* 306, no. 5702: 1776–80. Stutzer, Alois, and Bruno S. Frey. 2004. "Stress that Doesn't Pay: The Commuting Paradox." IZA Discussion Paper 1278. Bonn: Institute for the Study of Labor, August 2004.

The Public Health Benefits of Transit Investments

If improved infrastructure changed the way Americans live and work, there would be significant benefits to health and wellness. For example, MacDonald et al. find that improving neighborhood environments and increasing the public's use of light rail transit would benefit health to the extent it causes increased physical activity, a reduction in the incidence of obesity (body mass index greater than 30), and a reduction in the odds of becoming obese.[44]

Using data on individuals before (July 2006 to February 2007) and after (March 2008 to July 2008) the completion of a light rail system in Charlotte, North Carolina, they find that the use of light rail to commute to work is associated with a nearly 1.2 point reduction in body mass index as well as an 81 percent reduction in the odds of becoming obese. Moreover, improved perceptions of neighborhoods as a result of the availability of light rail were associated with 15 percent lower odds of obesity as well as higher odds of meeting weekly recommended physical activity levels for walking and vigorous exercise (9 percent and 11 percent, respectively).

In addition to all of the personal benefits associated with a healthier life style, overall costs on our health care system are substantially reduced when obesity rates are lowered, given that health care costs for the obese are almost twice the rate for normal weight individuals. Finkelstein et al. find that between 1998 and 2006, the prevalence of obesity in the United States increased by 37 percent, adding $40 billion dollars to health care costs.[45]

A separate study by Stokes et al. estimates that health care savings in Charlotte from the creation of the first segment of their light rail system could reach a cumulative $12.6 million by 2015.[46] These facts also suggest that targeted investment in creating new public transportation systems could translate into large-scale savings in health care costs. Furthermore, many other academic studies show that proximity to public transportation and more rationally-designed neighborhoods tend to be associated with increased walking and other physical activity for the general population, working or otherwise.

---

[44] MacDonald JM, Stokes R. Cohen D. Kofner A. Ridgeway G. The Effect of Light Rail on Body Mass Index and Physical Activity. American Journal of Preventive Medicine 2010; 39(2):105-112.

[45] Finkelstein EA, Trogdon JG Cohen JW Dietz W. Annual Medical Spending Attributable to Obesity: Payer- And Service-Specific Estimates. Health Affairs 28, no. 5 (2009): w822-w831.

[46] Stokes RJ, MacDonald J. Ridgeway G. Estimating the effects of light rail transit on health care costs. Heath Place 2008;14(1):45–58.

Safety

Failure to maintain our infrastructure network properly has significant consequences. For example, in August 2010, three major transportation systems in the Northeast corridor region (Amtrak, the Long Island Railroad, and New Jersey Transit) all experienced problems due to fire, power failure, and outdated equipment. Particularly illustrative of the need for upgrades of America's infrastructure was the fire in the Long Island Railroad's track switching system. Constructed in 1913, the system's breakdown forced rail personnel to switch tracks manually with mallets and spikes, an obviously outdated and hazardous practice.

Building a Safer and More Reliable Infrastructure System

The American people deserve safe and reliable infrastructure. Bridge collapses in recent years in Minnesota and Oklahoma remind us of the risk of neglecting our infrastructure and of unsafe designs. One in four bridges in the United States remains structurally deficient or functionally obsolete.

In 2006, motor vehicle traffic crashes were the leading cause of death for every person age 3 through 34. Though 2010 saw the lowest fatality and injury rates ever recorded, it is clear that we can still do better, as over 32,000 people died on American highways in 2010, or more than 90 people every day. Aging transportation systems – whether it is our roadways, transit systems, or railways – increase safety risks because they lack proven countermeasures that are installed on newer systems and equipment. Devoting resources to raising existing transportation infrastructure to a state of good repair in a "fix-it-first" approach is a sound strategy to help address critical safety challenges. The Federal Government, along with state, local, and private owners and operators of transportation infrastructure, must work together to target resources to risks before they become safety hazards.

A promising example of wise investment which can improve public safety is the installation of guard rails and cables along highways. One study examined a 14.5 mile stretch of highway between Dayton and Cincinnati over a three-year period after guard rails and cables were installed. Analysis of this data indicates that this investment could save more than 110 lives during the next twenty years, which equates to over 7 lives per mile of guard rail. Given the cost of installation of slightly under $90,000 per mile, this investment would more than pay for itself, if it saved only one life per year. While it is difficult to generalize as roadway conditions vary substantially, this study indicates that there may be significant potential to increase safety through additional targeted investment in guard rails and cables.

V.   Support for Infrastructure is Widespread

The merits of infrastructure investments must also be considered alongside projections of population growth, trading patterns, and expected changes in American lifestyles. As the economy and population grow, infrastructure resources will be stretched thinner as existing systems age and additional needs for new systems arise. With the U.S. population expected to grow to almost 440 million people by 2050 and interstate commerce expected to grow as well, targeted infrastructure investments can be one strategic tool that policymakers use to prepare for the future.[47]

American firms rely on infrastructure to enable efficient supply chain management and the transportation of goods to the point of sale. Investments in transportation infrastructure would allow firms in all 50 states to have the opportunity to benefit from growth in foreign markets. According to an analysis by the Brookings Institution, exports account for 8 percent of total U.S. employment[48]; smart investments in infrastructure have the potential to create more jobs in export-oriented U.S. companies. The President's National Export Initiative calls for the "Departments of Commerce and Transportation [to enter] into a Memorandum of Understanding to work together and with stakeholders to develop and implement a comprehensive, competitiveness-focused national freight policy. The resulting policy will foster end-to-end U.S. freight infrastructure improvements that facilitate the movement of goods for export and domestic use."[49] Moreover, the Department of Transportation "estimates that population growth, economic development, and trade will almost double the demand for rail freight transportation by 2035."[50] Export growth has been strong during the recovery. In 2011, exports were up over 33 percent from 2009, meaning that America is ahead of schedule in meeting the President's goal of doubling exports over 2009 levels by the end of 2014.

The business and labor communities have also expressed a desire for more transportation infrastructure investment. Proposals from the American Public Transport Association (APTA), the American Association of State Highway and Transportation Officials (AASHTO), the U.S. Chamber of Commerce, AFL-CIO, and the President's Council on Jobs and Competitiveness all call for greater infrastructure investment. APTA advocates for nearly $15 billion of investment for federal public transportation programs, and at least $2.5 billion to be put towards high-speed and intercity rail systems. AASHTO reported in 2009 that between $132 billion and $166 billion

---

[47] Department of Commerce. Bureau of Census. Current Population Reports. Population Projections of the United States by Age, Sex, Race and Hispanic Origin (Haver Analytics).
<http://www.census.gov/population/www/projections/usinterimproj/>.

[48] Katz, Bruce, Rothwell, Jonathan, Istrate, Emilia, "Export Nation", Brookings Institution, July 2010.

[49] "Report to the President on the National Export Initiative: The Export Promotion Cabinet's Plan for Doubling U.S. Exports in Five Years."National Export Initiative, 2010.
<http://www.whitehouse.gov/sites/default/files/nei_report_9-16-10_full.pdf>.

[50] "National Rail Freight Infrastructure Capacity and Investment Study." American Association of Railroads, 2007.
<http://www.camsys.com/pubs/AAR_RRCapacityStudy.pdf>.

of investment is necessary to rebuild and repair America's highways.[51] The view that more transportation infrastructure is necessary is consistent with other research, including the recently issued bipartisan report by two former Secretaries of Transportation, Norman Mineta and Samuel Skinner. Their report estimated that an additional investment of $134 billion to $194 billion per year is needed to maintain our transportation system, and an even larger sum, from $189 billion to $262 billion, would be needed to improve it.[52] The U.S. Chamber of Commerce has stated that "to have a transportation system that supports a 21st century economy, the United States needs a high level of investment targeted at improving performance across all modes and geographies. There can be no more business as usual."[53]

Support is widespread for reinstating Build America Bonds, particularly among state and local governments who were able to save their residents billions in lower borrowing costs as a result of BABs. The National Association of State Treasurers, the U.S. Conference of Mayors, the National League of Cities, the National Association of Counties, the Council of State Governments, and the National Association of State Auditors, Comptrollers, and Treasurers all endorsed bringing back BABs.[54] The Securities Industry and Financial Markets Association (SIFMA) also weighed-in in support of BABs, writing, "In recognition of its invaluable improvement in market structure and contribution to improving efficiency, liquidity and transparency for borrowers and investors alike, extending the BABs program would continue to provide these benefits to state and local governments."[55]

Americans Want Improved Infrastructure Capacity

American workers, families, and businesses are demanding more infrastructure investment. Americans have voted repeatedly for increased investment in transportation infrastructure with over 98 percent of the funds requested for transportation projects approved by the voting public in 2008.[56,57,58,59] A study by the Rockefeller Foundation found that four out of every five

---

[51] Oakley, Janet. "Investing in Transportation Infrastructure." Government Research Association Annual Policy Conference. American Association of State Highway and Transportation Officials. 29 July 2009. <http://www.transportation.org/sites/aashto/docs/Oakley-2009-07-28pdf.pdf>.

[52] Mineta, Norman, and Skinner, Samuel, "Well Within Reach: America's New Transportation Agenda"

[53] "Transportation Index National Results From 1990 to 2008." U.S. Chamber of Commerce. <http://www.uschamber.com/lra/transportation-index/national-results>.

[54] Letter to Senate Finance Committee, July 9, 2010.

[55] SIFMA letter to House Ways and Means Committee, March 23, 2010.

[56] Treasury calculations based on information compiled from [26], [27], and [28]. Where the funds were approved on an annual basis for an indefinite number of years, it was assumed that the measure was not extended beyond the initial year. The measures for which the total funding impact is ambiguous were excluded from this calculation.

[57] "2008 Transit Ballot Measures." Center for Transportation Excellence. <http://www.cfte.org/success/2006BallotMeasures.asp#2008CompletedTransitBallotMeasures>.

[58] "State and Local Ballot Initiatives." The Associated General Contractors of America. <http://www.agc.org/cs/State_and_Local_Ballot_Initiatives>.

[59] "NCSLnet Search Results: 2008 State Initiatives and Referenda." National Conference of State Legislatures. <http://www.ncsl.org/?tabid=13597>.

Americans agree with the statement that: "In order for the United States to remain the world's top economic superpower we need to modernize our transportation infrastructure and keep it up to date."[60] That study also found that the same proportion, 80 percent, agree that federal investment in infrastructure, "will boost local economics and create millions of jobs from construction to manufacturing to engineering." Another survey found that almost 19 out of 20 Americans are concerned about America's infrastructure and 84 percent support greater investment to address infrastructure problems.[61]

Evidence of this demand for greater transportation infrastructure and increased choice for alternatives forms of transportation is apparent in the sharp increase in transit ridership. Over the last 15 years transit ridership has grown by over 30 percent, reaching levels not seen since the 1950s.[62] This renaissance of transit ridership is in some ways a return to the past (see Figure 4).

---

[60] Rockefeller Foundation Infrastructure Survey, February 2011.
<http://www.rockefellerfoundation.org/news/publications/rockefeller-foundation-infrastructure-2>.
[61] "The Building America's Future National Survey," Luntz et al. 2009.
<http://bafuture.org/Websites/investininfrastructure/Images/Press%20Release%20memo2.pdf>.
[62] American Public Transit Association, Public Transportation Ridership Report

Figure 4.
Unlinked public transit passenger trips by mode

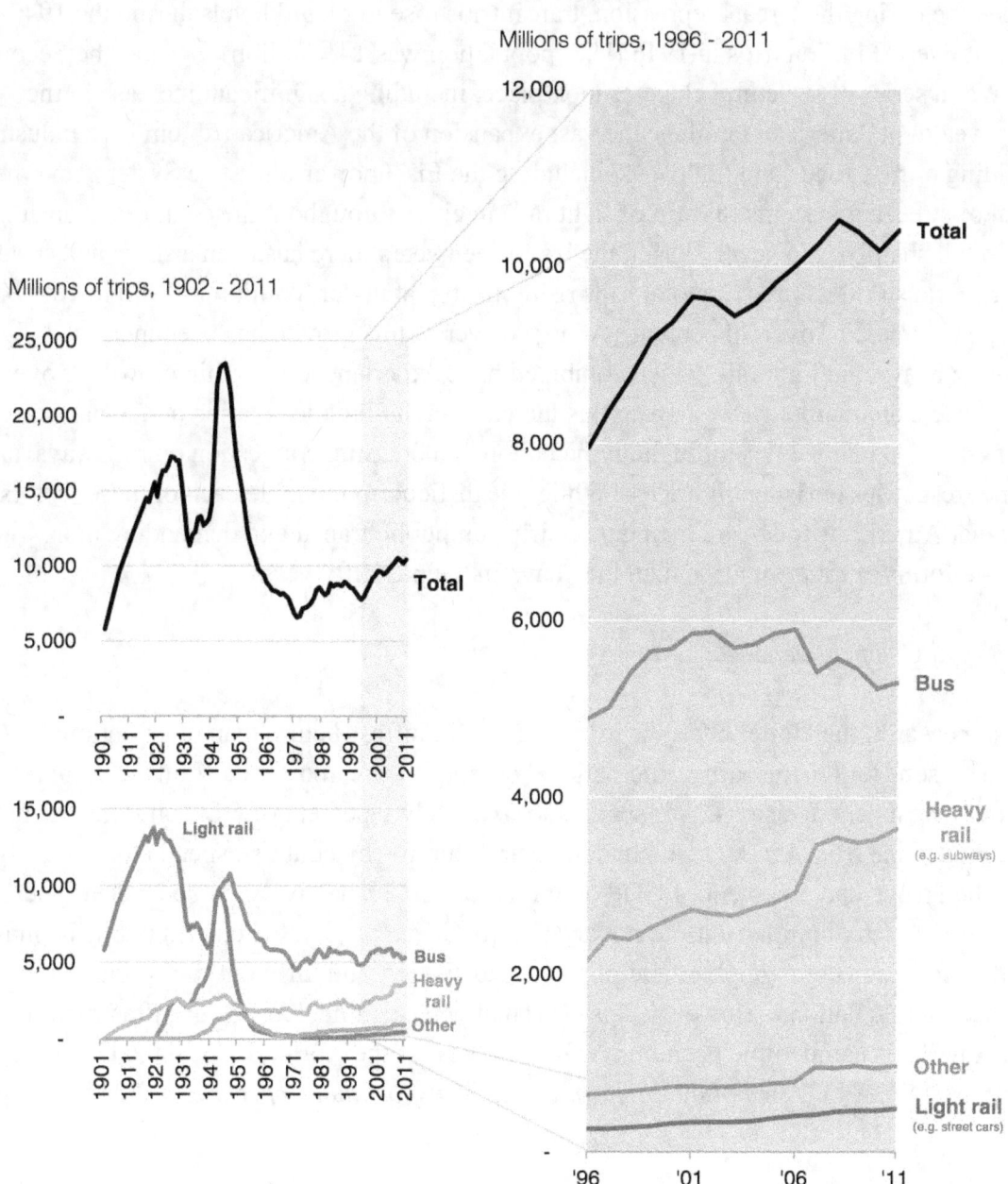

Millions of trips, 1996 - 2011

Millions of trips, 1902 - 2011

Source: American Public Transportation Association.

During the first half of the 20th century, transit systems were responsible for an astoundingly large number of total trips taken by Americans. Over 17 billion trips were taken annually on mass transit from 1926-1929 (U.S. population averaged approximately 120 million) and despite a sharp decline during the Great Depression, transit trips rose to record levels during the 1940s, peaking at over 23 billion trips in 1946 (U.S. population was 141 million).[63] After the Second World War a series of structural changes took place, including a significant increase in the average wealth of American families, the vast expansion of the American automotive industry, the building of new roads and highways, including the Eisenhower Interstate System, and the removal of street car systems (a form of light rail) in cities throughout the country. Transit ridership fell sharply. However, during the last fifteen years there has been a sharp and sustained increase in transit ridership, with total trips rising from just under 8 billion in 1996 to 10.4 billion in 2011, an increase of over 30 percent. A large driver of this growth has been increased ridership in heavy and light rail, which combined have experienced ridership growth of over 70 percent. There are many factors driving this increase, including the creation and expansion of transit systems in many cities throughout the nation,[64] increasing congestion on roadways, and consumer responses to rising oil prices. While it is difficult to untangle each of these factors, it is clear that Americans today are taking more trips on public transit and demanding more alternative forms of transportation than they have in the past fifty years.

International Competitiveness

By most measures, the United States is investing less in infrastructure than other nations. While there are reasons for this disparity, international comparisons can offer a useful benchmark to assess our investment decisions. We spend approximately 2 percent of GDP on infrastructure, a 50 percent decline from 1960.[65,66] China, India and Europe, by contrast, spend close to 9 percent, 8 percent, and 5 percent of GDP on infrastructure, respectively.[67] To be clear, these simple cross-country comparisons do not account for differences in the current public capital stock, differences in demographics and population densities, and different transportation preferences across nations. However, it is clear that persistent neglect of our infrastructure will impact America's competitive position *vis-à-vis* the rest of the world. Indeed, the U.S. Chamber of Commerce noted in their *Policy Declaration on Transportation Infrastructure* that, "Long-

---

[63] U.S. Census historical National Population Estimates

[64] New light rail lines and systems opened in at least 13 cities from 1996-2011: Dallas, Salt Lake City, Jersey City, Portland, Tacoma, Minneapolis, Houston, Trenton/Camden, Charlotte, Seattle, Oceanside, Phoenix, and Norfolk.

[65] Milano, Jessica. "Building America's 21st Century Infrastructure." Progressive Policy Institute, 15 January 2009. <http://www.ppionline.org/ppi_ci.cfm?knlgAreaID=450020&subsecID=900194&contentID=254788>.

[66] "Remarks by the President at CNBC Town Hall Discussion on Jobs" The White House Office of the Press Secretary, 2010. <http://www.whitehouse.gov/the-press-office/2010/09/20/remarks-president-cnbc-town-hall-discussion-jobs>.

[67] Ibid, and Royal Bank of India.

term underinvestment in transportation infrastructure is having an increasingly negative effect on the ability of the United States and its industries to compete in the global economy."

The Gallup World Poll indicates that compared to other OECD countries, Americans are relatively dissatisfied with their local public infrastructure systems (see Figures 5 and 6). Americans' satisfaction with highways and public transit ranks in the middle of the pack globally. With respect to our public transit, we are tied with four other countries at rank 13 out of 32 OECD nations. We rank similarly with respect to satisfaction with our roads and highways: 15th out of 32 OECD countries.

Figure 5.

Figure 6.

VI.   Conclusion

An analysis of the economic impact of transportation investment indicates that now is an optimal time to increase the nation's investment in transportation infrastructure. Investing in transportation infrastructure would generate jobs to employ workers who were displaced because of the housing bubble. We estimate that the average unemployment rate among those who would gain employment in the jobs created by additional infrastructure investment has averaged approximately 13 percent over the past twelve months. There is also accumulating evidence that construction costs are currently low because of underutilized resources, so it would be especially cost-effective to seize this opportunity to build the quality infrastructure projects that are ready to be built.

Historically, we also know that state and local governments are more prone to cut back on infrastructure spending during tough economic times, despite the growing need and demand for these projects. Americans overwhelmingly support increasing our infrastructure investment, as evidenced by consistent support for local investments on ballot initiatives. This is hardly surprising given that our report documents that the American public is less satisfied with our transportation infrastructure than residents of most other OECD nations.

Merely increasing the amount that we invest, however, must not be our only goal. Selecting projects that have the highest payoff is critically important, as is providing opportunities for the private sector to invest in public infrastructure. Given the significant need for greater investment, the federal government cannot, and should not, be expected to be the sole source of additional investment funds. More effectively leveraging federal investment by pairing it with state, local, and private investment is necessary to meet the challenges we face in expanding our transportation network. Thus, establishing a National Infrastructure Bank, along with other significant reforms in our infrastructure financing system, should remain a top priority.

Evidence also shows that well-functioning infrastructure systems generate large rates of return not only for the people who travel on the systems every day – the direct beneficiaries – but also for those in the surrounding regions and our nation more generally. Investment in infrastructure today will employ underutilized resources and raise the nation's productivity and economic potential in the future. By contrast, poorly planned, non-strategic investment is not only a waste of resources, but can also lead to lower economic growth and production in the future. That is why any increase in investment should be coupled with broad-based reform to select infrastructure projects more wisely. The President's proposal to increase our nation's investment in transportation infrastructure, coupled with broad-based reform of our transportation funding system, would have a significant and positive economic impact in both the short and long term, raising our nation's economic output, creating quality middle-class jobs, and enhancing America's global economic competitiveness.

VII. Appendix

Appendix Table 1:
Estimated Savings From Using Public Transportation - Selected Cities

Rank	City	Savings: Monthly	Savings: Annual
1	New York	$1,218	$14,618
2	Boston	$1,130	$13,559
3	San Francisco	$1,088	$13,060
4	Seattle	$995	$11,936
5	Chicago	$979	$11,744
6	Philadelphia	$976	$11,717
7	Honolulu	$939	$11,268
8	Los Angeles	$893	$10,712
9	Minneapolis	$890	$10,678
10	San Diego	$864	$10,369
11	Portland	$859	$10,312
12	Washington, D.C.	$861	$10,333
13	Denver	$857	$10,287
14	Baltimore	$843	$10,113
15	Cleveland	$828	$9,936
16	Miami	$802	$9,629
17	Dallas	$789	$9,472
18	Atlanta	$790	$9,480
19	Pittsburgh	$779	$9,347
20	Las Vegas	$763	$9,157

Source: American Public Transportation Association, Transit Savings Report, July 14, 2011. Based on a comparison of average monthly public transit costs and average monthly driving costs. For more detail see: <www.apta.com/mediacenter/pressreleases/2011/Pages/110714_Transit_Savings.aspx>.

Appendix Table 2:
Annual Vehicle Operating Cost in Selected Urban Areas

The twenty urban regions with at least 500,000 people (includes the city and its surrounding suburbs), where motorists pay the most annually in additional vehicle maintenance because of roads in poor condition:

Rank	Urban Area	Annual Vehicle Operating Cost
1	San Jose, California	$756
2	Los Angeles, California	$746
3	San Francisco – Oakland, California	$706
4	Honolulu, Hawaii	$701
5	Concord, California	$692
6	New Orleans, Louisiana	$681
7	Oklahoma City, Oklahoma	$662
8	San Diego, California	$654
9	New York – Newark, NY/NJ	$640
10	Riverside-San Bernardino, California	$632
11	Sacramento, California	$611
12	Tulsa, Oklahoma	$610
13	Indio-Palm Springs, California	$609
14	Baltimore, Maryland	$603
15	Omaha, Nebraska	$587
16	Kansas City, Missouri / Kansas	$587
17	San Antonio, Texas	$549
18	Dallas-Ft. Worth, Texas	$539
19	Detroit, Michigan	$536
20	Albuquerque, New Mexico	$527

Source: America's Roughest Rides and Strategies to Make Our Roads Smoother, Sept. 2010. <www.tripnet.org/urban_roads_report_Sep_2010.pdf>.

www.ingramcontent.com/pod-product-compliance
Lightning Source LLC
Chambersburg PA
CBHW081136280526
45787CB00007B/3105